Office Management,
Operations Management,
Crisis Management, and
Project Management
in Organizations

4 Management Topics in 1 Book

Louis Bevoc and Allison Shearsett

Published by
NutriNiche System LLC

I0494437

Office Management in Organizations

A Basic Introduction

Louis Bevoc

Published by
NutriNiche System LLC

Introduction

Office workers in organizations are responsible a variety of different tasks. They deal with human resource concerns and customer service issues. They also work with sales, marketing, and accounting personnel in order to keep businesses running effectively. Based on these responsibilities, it is rather obvious that their needs to be some type of supervision to make sure things get done efficiently and effectively...and that supervision is provided by an office manager.

Office managers oversee everything done in an office. If the office is small, they might have specific responsibilities in addition to supervision. For example, an office manager with two employees might handle the payroll while monitoring the job performance of the other two workers. However, in larger offices, office managers are often there only to supervise. For example, an office manager with 20 employees might not have any responsibilities other than supervising the action of those employees. In this type of a situation, office employees are often more skilled at their positions than their manager. Accountants and human resource professionals usually go to college to be trained in their profession, and this training gives them a solid understanding of the work they do. However, their efforts need to be managed and coordinated in order to benefit the entire organization.

Regardless of the size of the staff, office managers pay close attention to a diverse set of administrative tasks. However, they differ from the rank-and-file employees because they focus on outcomes and outputs so they can make changes for improvement.

Now that you have a basic understanding of the role that office managers play in organizations, let's move on to a discussion on the specific skills they need to do their jobs effectively.

Skills

This is an interesting topic for discussion due to the fact that office managers require such a wide variety of skills...and those skills not necessarily provided by formal education. Yes a college degree is helpful for managing an office, but it does not prepare people for the range of problems that they will encounter on a regular basis.

In small offices, learning often comes with experience. Experience is something that cannot be taught in a classroom or learned from a textbook. The "school of hard knocks" is often the best teacher, and those who cannot handle it probably should not pursue a career in small office management.

In large offices, office employees have specialized skills for their particular jobs. Those skills are the reason they were hired, and they are expected to utilize them for their work. Office managers would need degrees in several different areas to match the skills of all of their employees, but this is not practical and often times not beneficial. For example, an office manager who has an accounting degree would not find it useful for overseeing sales or marketing operations. Interestingly, if an office manager were to pursue a college degree, the best choice might be psychology since they have to deal with a lot of situations where psychological knowledge is useful.

So if college coursework is not necessary, then what skills are required for office managers? The answer lies in people's natural abilities. They must have good judgment and the ability to make decisions in pressure situations. Good judgment and decision making under pressure are important for keeping offices running smoothly due to the fact that change is constant. Office managers find themselves in situations where they need to decide what people should do and where they should go on a moment's notice...and those decisions are usually based on judgment.

Office managers also need to know how to organize and manage time wisely. Organization is critical for most aspects of business...especially when employees spend much of their day performing different job tasks as is the case in most offices. Time-management skills are necessary for making sure there are enough hours in the day to complete tasks that have been designated as important. Office managers who continue tell their boss that they "didn't have time" are usually replaced by people who are able to find that time and utilize it efficiently.

Two final skills that are necessary for office management are objectivity and the ability to multi-task. Objectivity is critical because people are being managed. If favoritism is paid to certain employees, then the entire office will suffer because employees will become less motivated to perform. Good office managers realize the potential fallout from a lack of objectivity, and they work hard to reduce any indication of bias. In additional to be objective, office managers also need to be able to multi-task. Without this ability, they simply will not get the things done that need to be accomplished. In busy offices, multi-tasking is often the single most important skill office managers possess because they need to oversee many worker activities at the same time.

In additional to having the above mentioned skills, office managers need to possess certain traits, abilities, and knowledge. Specifically, they must also be able interact socially and communicate with others, have a working knowledge of computers, and understand a little about finances. Each of these is broken down for better understanding as follows:

Social interaction

This ability is often underestimated in terms of importance. Office managers need to interact with a variety of different people inside and outside of the office, and this socialization has a significant impact on their jobs. When office managers are well-liked, they tend to get more accomplished. Unfortunately, the trait of socialization is not natural to everyone, and some office managers make a lot of enemies due to their "anti-social" behavior. However, the good news is that social graces can be learned...as long as the necessary time and effort are put forth.

Communication

This involves verbal and non-verbal communication. Office managers' actions, gestures, movements, expressions, and voice tone often speak louder than their words. They need to be aware of this and act accordingly when doing their job. Good commutation is essential for getting people to work together to accomplish tasks. It also prevents conflicts from escalating to a point where it is dysfunctional. When dysfunctional conflict occurs, the combatants focus on position instead of principle and personal attacks are often the result.

Computer knowledge

In today's business world, it is essential to have some understanding of computers. There is wealth of technology available, and much is found in offices of organizations all over the world. That being said, office managers must have some computer knowledge in order to succeed at their jobs. They do not need to be experts, but they should have a grasp on the programs and software used by the personnel they manage.

Financial knowledge

Office managers usually oversee different types accounting functions. In order to be efficient in this area, they should have some basic financial knowledge. They do not need to be experts, but they should be able to talk the lingo with the people in the various specializations that they manage. If they do not understand basic jargon, then they risk losing the respect of those who do.

Now you understand some of the basic skills necessary for office managers. Next, let's move into a discussion on their duties and job responsibilities.

Responsibilities

Office managers oversee a variety of different functions in organizations, and their duties can change based on the situation. For example, they sometimes need to buy office supplies, interview candidates for positions, prepare invoices, or answer telephones. All of these jobs fall under their jurisdiction, and they might need to do them if people are not in the office or they are tied up performing other tasks. However, they usually only fill in on a temporary basis because they are paid for being supervisors rather than workers. In short, office managers are responsible for making sure the office runs efficiently. That being said, the following are daily responsibilities they have in their roles as supervisors:

System support

Office managers are often charged with the responsibility of making sure the company computer system is functioning properly. They do not have to be able to troubleshoot computer problems, but they need to contact technical people if they are needed. These people can work for the company or as contract employees, but they need to be notified if there are computer issues in order to rectify the problems.

The job of overseeing system support is a bit of a thankless one. When computer problems occur, employees want them corrected immediately. They complain loudly when issues are not resolved to their liking, and those complaints resonate through the entire organization. Unfortunately, a quick fix is not always possible. Employees have to patiently wait to continue what they were doing, and this makes office managers look like they have failed...regardless of the reality of the situation.

Organizations pay a huge price when their computer systems go down. Productivity comes to a halt for many people's jobs, and the loss of their wages adds up quickly. There is also cost for getting systems up and running again. IT people are not cheap, and neither is the hardware or software required for repair. Office managers look bad even if the system is fixed because they are questioned about the expense after the bill arrives.

Personnel management

As noted in the introduction of this book, objectivity is a skill that office managers need to perform at maximum efficiency. They often supervise many employees, and they cannot afford to show favoritism to any person or group of people. However, regardless of how they choose to supervise, management of office personnel is their direct responsibility. When productivity suffers, office managers are viewed as not doing their jobs...and this could result in them being replaced.

Records

Much of the information about finances, sales, marketing, production, distribution, and employees is stored in offices. This information can be saved in hard copy form, but most of it is now saved electronically. Since this information is confidential, there is restricted access to it and passwords are necessary for people who are authorized. The protection of these records is the responsibility of office managers. They determine where the files will be stored and who has access to them.

The importance of this responsibility cannot be underestimated. Sensitive information such as employee pay or company profitability can create a variety of internal and external problems. In short, office managers who fail to guard records not doing their jobs properly.

Budgets

A common rule of businesses is that money affects virtually everything...and that rule applies to office management. Office managers cannot escape the financial boundaries put on their departments, and they need to work within those boundaries. They are directly responsible for the cost of keeping the office working efficiently and effectively.

In this role, office managers must document all hours worked by employees and keep track of other costs associated with maintaining the office. Supplies, office furniture, computer hardware, and software programs all fall into the cost category; and they need to be accounted for in the budget.

Goal setting

This responsibility is purposely saved for last due to its significance. Office managers need to set goals for their employees so they can reach milestones and view their accomplishments. These goals can be used for any tasks related to office work, but they should be:

Relevant

All office goals need to be relevant to those of the organization. For example, an office manager should not set a goal of reducing the office payroll by 20 percent over the next

8

year if management plans to double the number of people on staff in six months. A better goal would be related to efficiency, such as reducing the number of bookkeeping errors by 20 percent over the next year.

Transparent

This refers to understanding. Employees need to understand what the goals entail so they know what they need to do in order to be successful. This is best done with short meetings that address the details involved. Anyone who has ever worked for an organization with unclear goals knows how frustrating it can be to try to achieve them.

Attainable

This is probably the most aspect of goal setting. Goals need to be attainable, or it does not make sense to establish them. For example, a goal of completing 100 percent of all assigned tasks for the next two years is simply not possible. A better goal is the continuous improvement of task completion over the next two years, with an evaluation of progress every six months.

Now you understand some of the responsibilities of office managers. If they handle these responsibilities well, their efforts will benefit the organizations that employ them. This leads us to the next section that focuses on the advantages of office management.

Advantages

Office management offers organizations many benefits. It keeps organizations moving forward by addressing many of the tasks necessary to conduct everyday business, and it provides efficiency in areas where other departments fall short. The following are some specific advantages:

Administration

Office management is beneficial for organizations because it handles most administrative tasks. It supports people and departments by providing clerical work for supervisors, responding to customer concerns, administering employee benefits, and scheduling construction projects. Without office management these administrative functions would be pushed on the employees who already have full plates...and the end result would be lost efficiency and lower productivity.

Organization

People who have worked in unorganized businesses understand the stress that can result from these situations. Employees feel lost and unsure of the direction they need to take to accomplish job related tasks. Worse yet, they sometimes do not even know what it is that they are supposed to be attempting to accomplish. Office management helps keep businesses organized by designating specific needs and making sure those need are met. For example, office personnel need to make sure that all employees receive their chosen benefits in a timely and efficient manner. To successfully do this, they designate the required forms, pass them out to supervisors with instructions for completion, make themselves available to answer questions, and follow up until all of the forms are properly filled out and collected. This is a good example of the organization that office management provides.

Prioritization

Office management personnel lists tasks in order of importance, thereby making sure that the most pressing uses are the first to be addressed. If these types of decisions were left up to other departmental employees, they would most likely prioritize based on whatever is best for their individual needs. For example, office managers approve vacations for manufacturing employees. They make that workers do not schedule time off during high volume periods because the well-being of the company is more important than someone's individual needs. This might seem unfair to some people, but office management know it needs to be this way based on priorities.

Efficiency

Office management employees have a solid understanding of efficiency. They are hired to monitor costs and make sure organizations operate effectively. If something is not right, they make changes or notify the people who have the authority to take action. Office management personnel assume the role of watchdogs in organizations...and this makes those organizations more productive and efficient.

As you can see, there are some major advantages for having office management in organizations. However, there are also some negatives that need to be mentioned...and these negatives are discussed in the next section.

Disadvantages

As might be expected, there are some disadvantages associated with office management in organizations. These negatives do not outweigh the positives involved, but they need to be pointed out for a better understanding of office management as a whole. They are as follows:

Bureaucracy

Red tape is a problem for many organizations, and a lot of it can be found office management. Policies and procedures are often difficult to deal with for employees, and that difficulty is created and intensified by office management personnel. They often take something that is relatively simple and add complexity to it for legal or ethical reasons. This type of bureaucratic action upsets employees, and it will likely never change...which is precisely why it is a disadvantage of office management in organizations.

Multi-tasking

Multi-tasking is not something that is new to business. It is part of many people's jobs today, and has it been that way for many years. However, multi-tasking is taken to an entirely different level in office management. It is required for office managers because, without it, they would not be able to accomplish tasks and do their jobs. This is a disadvantage because sometimes the bar on multi-tasking simply cannot be raised any higher. When this happens, office management tasks to not get completed, and the organization ultimately suffers.

Inspiration

It is a challenge to motivate oneself...and it is even more challenging to motivate others. Office managers need to motivate their staffs to do their jobs, and this is not an easy task due to the mountain of paperwork and complexity of the work that is sometimes involved. Without motivation, office personnel are not as productive as they are capable of being...and that means some tasks do not get completed. In short, lack of inspiration is a negative associated with office management that end up hurting the organization as a whole.

Frustration

When people hit dead ends in their jobs, they often become frustrated. Unfortunately, this is all too common in office management. For example, office personnel who work on hiring seasonal employees for manufacturing positions are often not able to hire enough people in the time frame available. They make multiple phone calls and send out countless emails, only to find that people are not available to fill the need. The resulting frustration causes office personnel and managers to burn out...and the end result is a less efficient organization with production supervisors whose needs have not been met.

Now you understand some of the disadvantages associated with office management. These indicate there is room for improvement...and that is why improvement is the focus of the next section.

Improving

Not surprisingly, office management can be improved. It can be made more effective and efficient, thereby helping organizations become more successful. Progressive organizations are always looking to improve the management of their offices, and there are many different ways to do this. For example, the number of office employees might need to be increased or reduced...depending on specific needs. Offices that are short-staffed cannot get the work done that they are assigned. Additional people rectify this problem, thereby making the offices more productive. On the other side of the coin, offices that are over-staffed do not have enough work for employees, and this results in high labor costs. A reduction in personnel helps improve these offices by making them more efficient.

Some offices can be improved by updating outdated computer or office systems. Management needs to realize that these systems become archaic over time, and they eventually need to be replaced. Interestingly, money is not the only reason that organizations refrain from upgrading. Change also tends to be a factor because people avoid it like the plague. Employees do not want to leave their comfort zones and move on to something better due to the learning curve that is required and the uncertainty that comes with something new.

Unfortunately, there are cases where technology or staff cannot improve an office situation. When this happens, the blame usually shifts to the leadership. In other words, the manager who is unable to improve the office needs to be replaced by someone who is capable of doing so. This can be quite drastic in terms of impact on the staff...but it might be the only way to make a bad situation better.

All of the above suggestions for improvement work when something is wrong or out of balance. However, what about offices that are doing fairly well? Should they be improved or adhere to the "if it ain't broke don't fix it" mentality? The answer is they can and should be improved...and one way to do this is to implement a system called management by objectives (also known as MBO).

MBO was popularized by management guru Peter Drucker in the 1950s. The basic thinking behind this system was not originated by Drucker because it draws from the 1920s work of Mary Parker Follett. However, Drucker took MBO to a new level by applying it to organizations, and then one of his students (George Odiorne) published a book on it in the 1960s. Based on that book, businesses began to adopt the management processes and MBO as we know it today was born.

Essentially, management by objectives is a process that provides employees with direction by setting objectives. It defines roles and responsibilities while specifying a course of action, and the end result inspires employees to do their best and perform at optimum levels. This leads to the achievement of goals and objectives in an effective and time-efficient manner.

Based on the preceding paragraph, management by objectives appears to be the same as any top-to-bottom management structure. Leaders establish goals, responsibility for accomplishing those goals is given to lower level managers, and the rank-and-file employees perform the necessary tasks. However, MBO is different because management and employees work together. They agree on objectives and view them as a positive way to move forward. This type of thinking has potential for office management because employees usually understand their jobs and what needs to be done to meet the goals and objectives of their employer.

MBO is made up of the following major building blocks:

- *Systematic procedures*

    Procedures in MBO are methodical and orderly. This allows for maximum performance due to the structure involved. Employees are not left wondering what they need to do because their course of action has been pre-determined.

- *Systematic participation*

    Employee participation is a critical aspect of MBO. Without it, there would be no success as defined by the system. Employees are always involved in decision making, and their involvement motivates them to perform because they take possession of their jobs and the responsibility that comes with those jobs. This "process ownership" helps them identify with their organization and commit to its goals and objectives.

    Specific features of systematic participation include:

Responsibilities

Managers and employees must agree on job responsibilities. This means job duties are determined via a joint decision, and this process cannot be changed simply because the manager has more authority.

Goals

Managers and employees must agree on goals. This means goals are determined via a joint decision, and this process cannot be changed simply because the manager has more authority. These goals need to be realistic and attainable or MBO will not succeed. After the goals are established, managers assume a facilitation or coaching role where they offer employees support to help them succeed.

Methodology

Managers and employees must agree on methods for obtaining goals and evaluating the success of those goals. These methods are determined via a joint decision, and this process cannot be changed simply because the manager has more authority. Methodology often takes a back seat the actual goals because MBO is more concerned with what needs to be achieved rather than the process by which it is achieved.

- *Systematic planning and review*

    Organizations that incorporate MBO take planning to a new level. They work towards goals and objectives by evaluating results and rewarding the employees who have performed. Frequent changes to the plan are not uncommon because it is reviewed periodically rather than waiting until the end to make a determination. Feedback is important because it dictates the changes that need to be made.

In short, MBO is an all-encompassing management system that works toward achieving goals and objectives as effectively as possible. This system has potential to improve office management; and that is good news because office management needs to continually search for ways to get better in order to meet the growing needs of organizations.

Summary

Most organizations have an office that needs to be managed. This requires someone to take charge of people and process on a daily basis. This individual is "on the front line" with a variety of different responsibilities. He or she has to lead, organize, make decisions, and resolve conflict...and this is no easy task.

This book focuses on office management. First it examines the skills necessary to run an office, next it explores the responsibilities of office managers, then it discusses advantages and disadvantages of office management, and last it finishes with ideas for improvement. The text is information and educational, and it is written for easy understanding at all reader levels.

Congratulations! You now know more about office management...and important aspect of organizations all over the world.

Operations Management in Organizations

A Basic Introduction

Louis Bevoc

Published by
NutriNiche System LLC

Improving

Summary

Introduction

Every employee plays a role in helping organizations grow and prosper. Sales people sell products and services in order to generate revenue, marketing employees drive brand names of products and services, quality assurance personnel make sure products and services meet specifications, and accountants assure that money is available for financial needs. Operations managers also play a role, but their role is more encompassing than other employees. This is because they oversee a variety of different departments with the responsibly of making sure organizations run efficiently.

Operations management has strong roots in manufacturing. In fact, it used to be known as production management before the industrial revolution. The revolution sparked much more complex production, thereby forcing production managers to move into more specific responsibilities. At this point, operations management was born...and its importance continues to grow.

Today, operations managers work with all departments associated with production. They analyze work environments and implement improvement strategies. A good part of their job involves planning and organizing with a basic goal of making organizations more efficient and more profitable. They take action after inefficiencies are discovered by streamlining processes and procedures throughout the supply chain.

For this book, operations management is defined as:

> *Overseeing supply chain activities that increase the efficiency and profitability of organizations*

This definition gives a broad idea of the scope of operations management responsibilities, but it needs to be broken down for better understanding. Let's start by examining the skills necessary for operations managers.

Skills

As might be expected, the skills required for operations managers are quite diverse. After all, they are concerned with planning and organizing a wide variety of operational activities that involve materials, equipment, machines, transportation, technology, and people. They need to deal with many different issues throughout the supply chain, and the challenges involved can be detailed and complex. Based on these responsibilities, basic skills required for operations managers include:

Multitasking

This skill is fairly straightforward and simple to understand. Operations managers need to be able to multitask in order to perform at optimum levels. They work with a variety of different people and departments, and this requires juggling responsibilities so everything works out as efficiently as possible for organizations.

Understanding

This skill involves understanding organizational needs from all departmental perspectives and acting on those needs in an effective manner. It requires operations managers to know a little about a lot of different aspects of their organizations. Expertise is not necessary, but understanding is essential in order to make the right decisions. Sometimes this requires operations managers to "put themselves in other's shoes" to get a better understanding of the situations they are encountering. In terms of understanding, empathy is very important.

Communicating

Communication is important for every employee's job. However, it has particular importance for operations managers due to the number of people they need to deal with on a daily basis. Since these people differ in personalities and responsibilities, it is critical that operations managers know how to communicate effectively. It is also important to note that these communication skills need to be verbal, non-verbal, and written...depending on the situation.

Organizing

As noted in the introduction, operations management is "overseeing supply chain activities that increase the efficiency and profitability of organizations." This requires an understanding of all processes in order to get them to flow seamlessly and work effectively. People, processes, and materials need to be arranged in ways that help meet established goals and objectives...and this is difficult to do if operations managers do not possess organizational skills.

Problem solving

This might be the most important skill needed by operations managers because most of the work they do requires problem resolution. In fact, many times the only way to improve a process is to solve the problems that prevent it from getting better...which is much less time consuming and expensive than scrapping the entire process and starting from scratch.

Interestingly, some operations managers have to find problems by themselves before they can resolve them. People tend to get "tunnel vision" when they are involved with processes for long periods of time, and they are consequently unable to visualize what needs to be done to make them better. Operations managers provide a fresh set of eyes and, combined with their overall knowledge, are able to identify the problem areas and work towards resolutions.

Calculating

This refers to calculating numbers as support for decision making. These calculations can be simple, such as determining the square feet of manufacturing space; or they can be more complicated, such as using performance metrics to determine productivity. However, regardless of the complexity, operations managers need calculating skills to get their jobs done properly.

Now you understand some essential skills that are needed by operations managers. Let's expand upon this by discussing the accountability these individuals have in organizations....better known as their job responsibilities.

Responsibilities

Operations managers develop, organize, and improve people and processes while working toward strategic goals. They oversee many different aspects of organizations because they are concerned with efficiency and profitability. Based on this, they have a large number of diverse responsibilities. They usually do not physically perform the tasks related to these responsibilities, but they do oversee major aspects related to their development and progress.

The following are specific responsibilities assumed by operations managers.

Managing

As expected, operations managers are charged with managing people and processes. The following are some specific areas where they perform management functions within organizations:

Planning

This likely encompasses the majority of the management performed by operations managers. Planning is a rather broad category that includes personal and resources. People need to be put in the proper places and resources need to be utilized wisely. Planning also entails the financial aspects of organizations such as getting involved with the costs of raw materials or the labor costs of production.

Supervising

Operations managers need to directly supervise some personnel. Examples including telling manufacturing supervisors how to set up production lines, instructing engineers on equipment design, and directing quality personnel to uphold product specifications. Without this direct supervision, people are left to make decisions on their own...often times without the necessary ability or knowledge.

Reviewing

All organizations operate within designated boundaries. These boundaries are strict in some companies and much more lenient in others. However, they do exist in every organization functioning under a hierarchy...and they are commonly referred to as policies and procedure.

Operations managers review policies and procedures and alter them if necessary. This responsibility is often overlooked because many times nothing changes. For example, an inventory control procedure involving FIFO (first in, first out) could be reviewed by an operations manager and determined to be acceptable, so no changes are made.   However, changes that are made can have a major impact on the people and processes affected. For example, an operations manager might reduce the number of people on a production line from 21 to 18. This affects everyone on the line and can cause more anxiety for supervisors trying to reach production quotas.

Manufacturing

Operations management has its roots in production related activities, and those roots have never strayed too far. A core responsibility of operations managers involves making sure manufacturing related processes more effective and efficient. Manufacturing is a major part of operations management...and this will likely never change.

Maintaining

This refers to the maintenance of the machinery and equipment that is often found in factories or manufacturing plants. Operations managers work with engineers to assure equipment design is efficient, and they also work with maintenance people to assure machines operate properly. Maintenance is a critical aspect of production, and operations managers are charged with overseeing it.

Controlling

Operations managers need to control people and processes, and this control can be financial or physical. A financial example is keeping costs of project below a certain level. Costs that exceed that level must be approved by the operations manager or someone higher in the organization. A physical example is maintaining the quality of a product. Products that do not meet designated specifications are put on hold, and those products can only be released by the operations manager or someone higher in the organization.

Strategizing

This involves the planning and goal setting for everything along the supply chain. It incorporates management, materials, resources, manufacturing, distribution, and inventory into a strategy that drives organizations toward growth and prosperity. In this sense, operations managers are captains who guide ships toward efficiency and profitably.

A major part of strategizing includes what can be termed as "linking." Linking occurs when operations managers act as the major source of communication between two different departments. They make sure "one hand knows what the other is doing' by providing the guidance necessary to keep things running smoothly. Linking also occurs externally when operations managers communicate between their organizations and other organizations in the supply chain.

Now that you understand some of the more important job responsibilities of operations managers, it is time to move into discussion on the benefits of their efforts. The next section examines advantages of operations management.

Advantages

As noted earlier in this book, operations managers get involved with any aspect of the supply chain that needs to be made more efficient and profitable. This is important for every organization, but it has huge implications for those that compete globally. Operations managers understand trends in global supply chain management, methods for staying competitive, and ways to meet customer requirements. This is critical when costs escalate out of control, raw materials are short in availability, or customer demands reach new levels. That being said, operations managers offer advantages to organizations that include:

Profitability

From a textbook perspective, this is probably the biggest advantage that operations managers offer organizations. Businesses are established to make money; and operations management people aid in the quest to do so. Interestingly, this is often done by going against the status quo to make the necessary changes to become profitable. CEO's rely on operations managers to visualize what needs to be done and act accordingly. This means operations managers are at the top of the list of important employees...and they are worth their weight in gold.

Technology

It is widely understood by people in business today that technology is critical for moving forward. Operations managers are often competent in terms of technology...especially when it comes to manufacturing. For example, they understand the computer-aided design software that can be used for production, and they also are familiar with the bar coding technology that can be used for inventory control. In short, they have the knowledge required to make processes more efficient from start to finish while reducing costs.

Objectivity

Operations managers are able to objectively look at processes and procedures and make changes because they are not mentally, emotionally, or physically tied to the processes. Their role is to step back and implement constructive changes based on their observations. In this capacity, they are not bias and make decisions based on what it best for the organization in terms of efficiency and profitability.

Without operations managers, employees become complacent and view things from their own individual perspectives rather than looking at the big picture. When operations managers make objective decisions, they often take people out of their comfort zones. This is because those decisions are made in the best interests of organizations rather than individual workers or departments.

Compliance

Every organization has some type of government regulations that they need to abide by, and these regulations are quite numerous when the entire supply chain is taken into consideration. Operations managers analyze policies, processes, and procedures and understand what they need to do to prevent the government from stopping production or issuing fines for violations. They are actively involved in implementing internal controls to make sure the actions of their organizations follow the required laws. For example, operations manager are proactive on food safety for meat processing plants. This action prevents the USDA (United States Department of Agriculture) from intervening and taking disciplinary action that can be as severe as mandating a product recall.

Support

On the surface, it might appear that the changes operations managers make in organizations are hard on employees. After all, those changes require employees to undergo change that is difficult due to uncertainly and fear of the unknown. However, operations managers also help calm employees by providing support for them. They do this by establishing direction and engaging workers in the process. Once engaged, employees take ownership of the tasks associated with their jobs and perform at optimum levels.

Support is critical for certain types of employees. In fact, some workers are unable to motivate themselves and need help from people in higher positions (such as operations managers) in order to do their jobs to the best of their ability. In short, the support provided by operations managers helps employees find comfort and is therefore beneficial to organizations.

Benchmarking

Benchmarks are standards that organizations strive to reach. They are used to raise the bar for current practices with the ultimate goal of continuous improvement. When properly utilized, benchmarking is an excellent tool for increasing performance and productivity. It helps organizations grow and prosper as they compete in markets that are constantly undergoing change.

Organizations that use benchmarks are searching for best practices. They compare their processes and procedures to leading practices in their industry and attempt to raise their own standards. Essentially, the benchmark they choose provides them with a snapshot of where they are and where they want to be. This process is never-ending because practices need to be constantly re-evaluated to monitor position and progress...and that is why there is a goal of continuous improvement.

Operations managers use benchmarking to make strategic decisions. They are able to measure critical functions of the workplace and make adjustments. Those adjustments are then monitored to make sure they are working to better the organization as a whole.

When properly executed, benchmarking is a great driver for organizational change. It exposes weaknesses and areas that require improvement using data that was collected and analyzed under a pre-designated plan of action. The results of benchmarking often make people uncomfortable, but sometimes individuals need to leave their comfort zones in order to better themselves and their organizations.

Fresh perspective

This advantage expands upon the objectivity benefit where operations managers take a step back and implement changes based on what it best for their organizations. This prevents employees from becoming complacent and seeing things only from their own perspective. Operations managers provide a new set of eyes that view an organization as a whole rather than individual parts competing against each other for success. Perception is people's reality...and employees who perceive something a certain way often have trouble seeing it differently. Operations managers provide a fresh perspective that sees things from an efficiency and profitability point of view...thereby leading to necessary change.

Competitiveness

Competition is the one of the best and worst aspects of business. This might appear to be a contradicting statement, but it is true. Competition drives some organizations to get better, but it also puts others out of business. It keeps organizations healthy, but it also makes employees sick. It motivates some employees to work harder, but it also causes others to give up. In short, competition is a double-edged sword.

Operations managers play a big role in competition because they encourage competitiveness while motivating employees to perform at peak levels. They understand competitor strategies and work to overcome those strategies within their own organizations. They do this by implementing internal strategies and guiding their employees toward the goals and objectives necessary to accomplish those strategies. In a sense, this advantage expands upon the support benefit discussed earlier.

As you can see, there are many advantages to operations management in organizations. However, there is also a downside to this profession...and that is why the next section focuses on disadvantages.

Disadvantages

It would not be fair to write about operations management without discussing some of the negatives it brings to organizations. Although these negatives are fairly limited, they can occur because operations managers do not always produce the expected results.

Specific disadvantages of operations management include:

Creativity and innovation

Creativity and innovation are often thought of as identical. They are linked, but they are not the same. The following are definitions of these two concepts as related to organizations:

Creativity

This is the process of associating thoughts and ideas with each other in order to create something that is potentially useful for organizations. Innovation is fueled by creativity in workplaces.

Innovation

This is the process of putting creativity into action and adding value to organizations. Creativity needs innovation in order to be useful in workplaces.

Innovation adds value to workplaces by harnessing creativity and making it useful. Some innovation appears to be serendipitous, but it usually stems from employees' hard work. Without innovation, organizations fail to grow beyond their current status...and sometimes this leads to their unfortunate demise.

Operations managers take control of situations by placing employees in positions that are best for organizations. This is good in many instances, but it also stops workers from coming up with new ideas and concepts. Decisions are made for them, and this decreases their desire and ability to produce the creative thoughts that fuel innovation.

Short-term sacrifices

Organizations need to understand that operations management is an investment for the future. Unfortunately, this is not always the case. Some companies weigh the money spent against immediate accomplishments, and the bottom line rarely looks good. Payback from operations management typically comes after strategies have had time to mature and produce results. Short term sacrifices need to be made when operations managers are hired...and this is something that many organizations have difficulty comprehending.

Cost

The mighty dollar is something that organizations must take into consideration when making decisions. Cost is a factor for virtually every aspect of business, and this includes operations management. Operations managers require a financial commitment that some organizations simply cannot afford. If this is the case, then employees are forced to wear multiple hats and operations management functions are limited.

Unfortunately, some organizations take the leap and hire operations managers when they cannot afford to do so; and they focus on the upfront costs rather than the benefits that will transpire later on. Companies that try to equate wages with immediate accomplishments typically end up quite frustrated...and they eventually see the hiring of operations managers as a lost cause. In short, the cost of operations managers can have a negative impact on organizations if the money is not there to support the objectives of the job.

As you can see, there are some disadvantages to operations management. Let's expand on this by discussing challenges in the next section.

Challenges

Disadvantages of operations management are somewhat limited, but this profession is not short of challenges. Please consider the following:

Social responsibility

Social responsibility is the obligation of organizations to make sure that there is a balance between their economy and the environment. In other words, profitability is not the only concern. Operations mangers sometimes find it difficult to put any aspect of business on the same level as financial success because, after all, profitability is a major part of their jobs.

Money drives organizations because, without it, those organizations would cease to exist. However, it has been suggested that social responsibility leads to profitability because many socially responsible thoughts and ideas are generated by the public...and companies that ignore those thoughts and ideas have difficulty selling their products and services to the public.

Organizations become socially responsible avoiding any type of socially harmful actions and by doing things that directly advance socially responsible goals and objectives. This is challenging for operations managers because now they have another factor to take into consideration when making decisions. They can no longer base strategic planning only on profitability and efficiency.

Capacity

This refers to the amount of responsibility that can be handled by operations managers. Everyone has breaking points where they simply cannot do any more...and this certainly holds true for operations managers. They have a wealth of responsibility, and adding more to their plate can cause their effectiveness to diminish. In short, the work-load capacity of operations managers can be challenging because it has the potential to limit their effectiveness.

Corporate

This refers to the issues created by corporate leadership. Operations managers have bosses, and those bosses need to be satisfied with the work being performed. However, corporate leaders often sit in "ivory towers" that are far away from the daily battles fought by rank-and-file employees. Higher-up management decisions are sometimes made without taking everything into account, and operations managers are left to clean up the resulting problems. This can be challenging...especially if corporate personnel have a tendency to micromanage.

Communication

As noted earlier in this book, communication is important for operations managers due to the number of people they interact with on a daily basis. Good operations managers have a natural ability to communicate, but that ability can be challenged if the need for commutation becomes overwhelming. No employee can be everywhere they need to be all of the time...and this means operations managers can find it challenging to communicate their messages to everyone involved.

Perception

Reputation follows an organization wherever it goes. It helps some companies to grow and prosper, while it forces the closure of others. If people see a company where greed drives executives at the expense of others, then they think negatively about that organization. Reputation is an important part of perception that is driven by the actions of organizations.

Operations managers need to rise to the occasion and overcome the negatives of perception regardless of the intensity. This is truly a challenge that operations managers face...and they must put serious thought into how their decisions impact that challenge.

Training

Training is significant for many organizations because it offers a wide variety of advantages. These advantages include improved worker skills, higher job satisfaction, increased employee motivation, and better teamwork. That being said, operations managers sometimes need to incorporate training into their ideas for improvement; but this is often easier said than done. Trainers need to be brought in, dates and times need to be established, and mediums (web-based, webinars, on the job, meetings, etc.) need to be determined. These requirements are difficult to control for operations managers....and it is why training presents a challenge.

The challenges faced by operations managers are plentiful, but they need to be overcome if organizations are to be successful. This is done by improving operations management as a whole...and it takes us to the next section on improvement.

Improving

Operations managers help organizations achieve goals and objectives. Their performance directly impacts efficiency and profitability, so it is relatively easy to understand that they need to be constantly searching for ways to get better. The following are some suggestions for improvement:

Plan

Leaders of organizations tend to hire operations managers before fully thinking through the responsibilities of the position. This is not good because operations managers are like any other employee...they need some type of direction. They are hired to organize and lead...but they have difficulty doing this without some type of plan in place that includes goals and objectives. In short, organizations must be proactive instead of reactive in terms of hiring operations managers.

Invest

Most good things in life require some sort of investment or they will not function as anticipated. This is true for most aspects of business, including operations management. Resources need to be allocated for implementing, maintaining, and improving the profession; and these resources are more than just financial. Feedback and guidance are necessary for motivating operations managers to perform at high levels in order to make decisions that are best for organizations. Lines of combination must be open for better understanding of problems that require immediate attention and issues that can be addressed at a later time. In short, change is constant in organizations, and operations managers need to be aware of those changes so they can adjust their words and actions. leaders need to understand that time and money spent now can prevent a lot of time and money from being spent in the future.

Lead

Astute managers hold themselves accountable for their actions and avoid blaming others. Operations managers need to establish a vision and take responsibility for making sure employees are working toward that vision. This requires delegation and monitoring to make sure tasks are getting completed. In short, operations managers must lead rather than play the blame game. They are charged with establishing organizational direction, and they need to make sure employees are doing the things necessary to achieve the related goals.

Listen

This method of improvement is often not given the credit it deserves. Operations managers need to listen to the things employees are saying about the day-to-day activities of organizations. Many times this can only be done by asking questions because workers do not always volunteer information.

The key to listening is communication. Operations mangers need communicate with employees to determine the things that need to be done and the roadblocks that need to be overcome. Listening leads to the implementation of ideas and concepts that prevent a wealth of problems down the line.

Act

Leaders of organizations need to prevent operation manager stress and burnout, and they can do this by showing concern and support through positive actions. For example, rather than telling an operations manager that employees need training for a new procedure, leaders should have a qualified trainer ready at a moment's notice. This alleviates the responsibility of finding a trainer for the operations manager, and it shows support for him or her. In short, actions speak louder than words...and leadership actions speak much louder than their rhetoric.

Summary

Operations managers analyze work environments and implement improvement strategies. They plan and organize with a basic goal of making organizations more efficient and profitable. They work toward eliminating inefficiencies and streamlining processes and procedures throughout the supply chain.

This book focuses on operations management in organizations. First it examines the skills and responsibilities of operations managers, then it analyzes the advantages and disadvantages of the profession, and last it explores challenges in the field and methods of improvement. The text is informational and educational, and it is written for easy understanding at all reader levels.

Congratulations! You now understand more about operations management...an important aspect of organizational growth and prosperity.

Crisis Management
in Organizations
Using Real World Examples

Allison Shearsett and Louis Bevoc

Published by
NutriNiche System LLC

Introduction

Organizations that face harmful happenings need to react in ways that minimize or eliminate the danger...and the process by which they do this is commonly known as crisis management. Before going any further, it is important to discuss the makeup of a crisis. For the purposes of this book, an organizational crisis is defined as:

> *Unanticipated events, behavior, or activities that threaten the well-being of organizations and employees*

What are the basic features of a crisis? First, a crisis typically comes with little or no warning. This means that there is usually no official start time or time for preparation. Second, a crisis brings about fear in employees. This fear can be very serious...even to the point where some people fear for their lives. Third, management understands that a reaction is necessary. They are aware that sitting back and doing nothing will only make the situation worse.

Crisis management is a defense system used by management for preventing, controlling, and/or terminating situations involving a crisis. This system differs from risk management because risk management works to avoid threats while crisis management is applied after the threat has materialized. Crisis management replaces the normal day-to-day system after it is no longer effective...typically before, during, and after a dangerous situation.

Organizations typically have crisis management programs in place for emergency situations. These programs designate responses that will resolve the problems involved. The responses are important because the reputation and credibility of organizations are influenced by the way they respond to a crisis.

Now that you have a basic idea of what defines a crisis and the reasoning behind crisis management programs, let's move into a discussion on specific types of crisis situations.

Types

This refers to the different kinds of crises that occur in organizations. Specific types include:

Ethical misconduct

Ethics violations occur in organizations all over the world, and certain types of ethical misconduct can lead to crisis situations. Bribery is an example of this, and one only needs to look at the not so distant Wall Street scandals to understand the problems that ethics can create. Ethics are part of a moral compass that guides people...but sometimes it guides them in the wrong direction.

Illegal activity

Organizations that engage in illegal activity create the perfect storm for a crisis. One example is a company not paying taxes on money earned, another example is a company involved in collusion, a third example is the formation of a monopoly, and the fourth example is a company influencing the price of their stock by buying or selling it at predetermined times (sometimes based on insider information). There are many ways that illegal activity can occur, but the common denominator of all of these is the fact that they can trigger a crisis.

Technological or mechanical failure

Downed computers systems, power failures, and equipment or machinery malfunctions are all examples of technological or mechanical failures that can lead to a crisis. This type of crisis has grown in occurrence more than any other in recent years due to the dependence organizations have on technology. Some companies are virtually brought to a halt without computer generated information. An example is a company that designs websites. If their technology is lost...then so is their business.

Financial problems

Financial issues can surface for a variety of reasons including reduced sales, theft, embezzlement, government intervention, and union strikes. If a money problem becomes too big to handle, then a crisis can result. Interestingly, some money problems result from short-term thinking that could be avoided. An example involves profitability. When immediate profit takes priority over everything else, long-term growth often gets cast aside...and companies experience financial issues that lead to a crisis.

Workplace violence

Conflict between coworkers occurs in every organization, and this is likely never going to change. Conflict that is functional is constructive because different experiences, viewpoints, and opinions are used for problem solving. However, dysfunctional conflict is not good....and it can turn violent. Violent conflict can escalate and turn in to a crisis in a very short period of time.

Workplace violence can also come from external sources. Jilted spouses, unpaid debts, and revenge have all been known to trigger physical attacks. Emotions such as jealousy, anger, and frustration can all cause violent reactions...and that violence can occur in organizations.

Terrorism

Any act of terrorism creates an instant crisis situation. This includes hostage situations, physically harmed personnel, computer hacking, food contamination, water contamination, and air contamination. This type of crisis results from purposeful actions that are designed to gain some compliance, show strength, or make a point.

Natural Disasters

Natural disasters are also known as "acts of God." They consist of tornadoes, earthquakes, fires, tsunamis, hurricanes, and other uncontrollable aspects of nature. They do not always result in a crisis, but they certainly have the ability to do so. For example, a lightning strike that ignites fire in an outside dumpster does not constitute a crisis, but a crisis could arise if that fire spreads to an office building.

Miscommunication

Miscommunication can be blamed for many different problems in organizations...including crises. One employee misinterpreting what another has said might be relatively harmless, but it could also lead to a crisis. For example, an employee joking tells two coworkers that an angry coworker is carrying a gun. The two coworkers do not interpret the humor as intended, and they put the entire workplace into a panic mode. The police are contacted, the building is evacuated, and work ceases for the remainder of the day. Based on this, it is relatively easy to understand how miscommunication can lead to crisis situations.

Now that you understand the basic types of crises that can occur in organizations, let's move on to a discussion on the implementation of a crisis management program using real world examples.

Programs

This section explains how crisis management programs are developed and written. It lists essential steps that must be adhered to, and it includes a food processing company example for each step. The program consists of two parts, *before the crisis* and *after the crisis*, as follows:

Before a crisis

The following steps need to be taken before a crisis occurs using a food processing company as an example.

1. *Create a team*

    This entails putting together a team of skilled individuals who will be in charge of all aspects of the program and handle crisis situations when they occur. The team does not need to be all management personnel, and it can include outsiders.

    Example: The food processing company sets up a team that consists of the production manager, quality manager, union steward, purchasing agent, controller, and a company attorney. This group is well-rounded and should understand the most important needs of the organization. Work phone numbers, cell phone numbers, and emails are listed so there is 24/7 access to these individuals.

2. *Define the worst*

    Never underestimate the potential for a crisis and plan accordingly. This means being proactive rather than reactive...and it starts with brainstorming. The crisis management team needs to meet and think about potential crises that could occur. Once these thoughts are established, possible responses can start to be formulated.

> **Example #1:** The food processing company thinks about tornados, fires, workplace violence, computer hacking, ethical violations, illegal activity, strikes, layoffs, and financial difficulties. The company is located in the Midwest, so earthquakes, tsunamis, and hurricanes are not a major concern.

Although this is rare, some crises can be planned for in advance.

> **Example #2:** The food processing company knows in advance that they are closing their bakery division. This structural move will put some employees out of work...and it could cause a panic throughout the organization. The crisis management team thinks about what could happen in terms of panic. Will there be a union strike? Will key people leave the organization? Will morale and motivation be negatively impacted? All of these questions are brought into the open for discussion.

3. *Establish a spokesperson*

Someone on the crisis management team needs to be the designated contact for the outside world for any type of crisis. This person should be able answer questions from suppliers, customers, government, the public, and the press. It might be tempting to designate multiple people for this role, but that is typically not a good idea. People say different things and their words could contradict each other, thereby making a bad situation even worse.

> **Example:** The food processing company designates their attorney as the spokesperson. This individual is a skilled writer and speaker, and she is experienced at answering questions in difficult situations.

4. *Identify proper authorities*

This designates the authorities that will be contacted when a crisis occurs. People from these organizations are experienced with crisis situations, and they can provide assistance and advice.

> **Example:** The food processing company generates the following list of authorities that will be contacted:
>
> - Police and Fire Department
> - Water Department
> - Alarm Company
> - Rescue/Ambulance: 911
> - FBI

- Department of Homeland Security
- Government Agencies: USDA, FDA, and OSHA

5. *List potential crises*

This defines the potential crisis that could occur. It takes the thoughts from the brainstorming (*define the worst* section) sessions and reduces those thoughts to real possibilities.

Example: The food processing company generates the following list of potential crises:

- Fire – natural, accidental, or arson
- Raw material contamination – water, food ingredients (accidental or purposeful)
- Finished product contamination – accidental or purposeful (sabotage)
- Workforce shortages – planned (strike, walkout, etc.) or unplanned (illness, transportation, etc.)
- Power failure – planned (sabotage) or unplanned (faulty equipment or energy loss)
- Weather (rain, tornadoes, snow, etc.)
- Chemical spills (cleaning, sanitizing, maintenance, etc.)
- Governmental – food safety (USDA), workplace safety (OSHA), or financial violations (IRS)

6. *List actions taken*

This designates what will be done when a crisis occurs. The specific crisis is identified along with the actions that will be taken.

Example: The food processing company designates the following actions for a power failure:

- Provide flashlights to management personnel
- Check for trapped people in all areas (processing areas, elevators, stairways, etc.)
- Evacuate the building (if necessary)
- Call emergency contacts as determined necessary (refrigeration contractor, electrician, electric and gas companies, etc.)
- Conduct an onsite inspection to determine where outage exists, and try to find out when power will be restored
- Shut down all equipment that could be damaged
- Cover exposed product and keep all cooler/refrigerator/freezer doors closed
- Monitor products for food safety concerns

- Document all injuries/incidents/expenses incurred

7. *Train affected personnel*

> Normally, this means training the members of the crisis management team. However, all employees might require some type of training process in order to educate them on the potential for a crisis, the actions taken during a crisis, and the effects of a crisis.
>
>> **Example:** The food processing company holds an annual training session with the crisis management team. An outside consultant facilitates the meeting and gears the content toward specific needs of the company. A test is given at the end of the meeting and all team members must answer 100 percent of the questions properly, or they are retrained and retested until they fully comprehend the subject matter.

After a crisis

The following steps need to be taken after a crisis occurs using the food processing company as an example.

8. *Assess*

> This refers to assessing the damage that was done during the crisis. Questions that need to be answered include: Was equipment damaged? Was product damaged? Was property damaged? Were people injured?
>
>> **Example (for a fire):** A fire occurred at the food processing company's pasta plant. All of the equipment in the packaging area was destroyed, but the rest of the plant had little damage. Fortunately, nobody was injured.

9. *Gather feedback*

> After a crisis is over and done, management needs to gather information. This information can be used to understand better why the crisis occurred, and it can potentially be used to prevent a reoccurrence.
>
>> **Example (for a fire):** The food processor asks questions about the fire to police and fire investigators. Fire investigators determine that the problem came from faulty wiring. The means terrorism and sabotage can be ruled out, and it also means electricians need to take appropriate action to prevent this from happening again.

Crisis management programs are designed to combat any type of crisis, but they are not foolproof. Something can go wrong or the plan simply might not work. Whatever the case, these programs often have weaknesses....and those weaknesses are discussed in the next section.

Weaknesses

Below are weak points of crisis management programs that often render those plans ineffective.

Before a crisis:

The following are weak points of crisis management programs before a crisis occurs using the food processing company as an example:

- *Importance*

   This might be the most common weakness. It occurs when programs are not considered important to top management. If this is the case, then these programs will not be taken seriously by employees, and they could fail when needed.

   Example: Assume the CEO of the food processing company does not get involved with the crisis management program. He tells his vice presidents to implement the program, and they pass the responsibility on to their managers. There is no commitment from upper management, so the crisis management team does not place a high level of importance on the program. It is thought of as just another directive from upper management...so the team merely goes through the motions of implementation.

- *Brainstorming*

   This refers to a lack of effort given to thinking about crisis situations that could occur. All potential crises need to be taken into consideration, and this requires some serious brainstorming. Crisis management teams that take this responsibility lightly could be headed for big problems later on.

   Example: The production manager, quality manager, union steward, purchasing agent, controller, and company attorney make up the food processing company's crisis management team. Assume that the lawyer and controller are "too busy" to make it to the brainstorming meetings. Their absence means potential financial and legal crises are not being considered...and this means that the other member's brainstorming is incomplete.

- *Application*

This refers to a crisis management program being too generic. It happens when organizations fail to tailor a program to their individual needs.

> **Example:** Assume the crisis management team at the food processing company obtains a crisis management program from the internet that uses an automotive manufacturer as an example. This is a good start since manufacturing is a common dominator. However, the team fails to modify the program to meet the needs of their company. For example, the automotive program has a heavy focus on machinery and equipment crises that can occur on the manufacturing floor. This is applicable to the food processing company, but they need most of their focus to be on food safety...something the automotive manufacturer does not take into consideration.

- *Delegation*

This weakness occurs when responsibilities of crisis management teams are not designated. Team members are unsure of what they need to do because nothing has been delegated.

> **Example:** Assume the food processing company selects the team members, but does not assign responsibilities to any of them. This creates confusion and fighting over who will do what...and eventually everyone stops communicating. In short, the program has failed before it has a chance to get off the ground.

- *Clarity*

This weakness occurs when responsibilities of crisis management teams are not clearly designated. This differs from the delegation weakness because team members are told what they need to do, but they not given any details. In other words, the assigned responsibilities lack clarity.

> **Example:** Assume all members of the crisis management team at the food processing company have been assigned responsibilities. The purchasing agent has been charged with making sure money is available for any type of crisis. However, she is left confused for because no other direction is given. How much money should be available? Where does this money need to be held? Who should have access to this money? When should the money be released? Nothing has been clarified, so there is ample room for misunderstanding and confusion.

- *Communication*

This weakness should not come as a surprise to anyone who has worked for a business. Communication is critical for efficient operation of virtually every aspect of business, and crisis management in no exception. Without good communication, crisis management programs fail to be successful...before or after the crisis.

> **Example #1:** Assume the crisis management team at the food processing company is established by upper management. Individual responsibilities have been assigned, and implementation of the program seems to be going fairly well. However, team members are not communicating with each other. Each member has some good ideas, but they do not discuss those ideas as a group. There is no defining of potential crises or documentation of actions that will be taken because the team does not meet regularly for discussion. Eventually, the crisis management program is abandoned due to what appears to be a lack of interest...but the problem actually stems from a lack of communication.

A crisis management program can also fail due to lack of commutation with the outside world. During a crisis, outsiders such as police and firefighters need to be contacted to help resolve the problem. If there is a lack of communication with outsiders, then the program will not be successful

> **Example #2:** Assume the food processing company finds out that a broken water main has caused a "boil alert" for their sausage manufacturing plant. They go into crisis mode and do not make any sausage products with the contaminated water. After the water is deemed safe by local authorities, they go back to normal production. However, they did not contact the United States Department of Agriculture (USDA) about the problem. When an inspector arrives, she condemns all sausage made during the crisis because USDA was not notified. The sausage cannot be released for sale to the public due to a lack of communication with an outsider.

- *Training*

"Practice makes perfect" is a saying that has been around for many years. It can be applied to crisis management programs because, without practice, these programs will most likely fail when they are needed most. This practice comes in the form of training that prepares employees for crisis situations that could take place. Unfortunately, many organizations with solid crisis management programs fail to train...and they are not prepared for emergency situations.

> **Example:** Assume the food processing company has a good crisis management program in place. They take a generic program and tailor it to their specific needs, but they fail to implement any type of training. They do not conduct practice runs, so people are unsure of what they need to do when a real crisis occurs. This lack of training jeopardizes the value of the crisis management program, and it reflects poorly on the leadership of the organization.

After a crisis

The following are weak points of crisis management programs after a crisis occurs using the food processing company as an example:

- *Evaluation*

    Some organizations fail to assess the damage done after a crisis has occurred. Evaluation is critical because it puts a cost on the crisis...and high costs are great motivation for taking the necessary steps to prevent the same crisis from happening again.

    Example: Assume the food processing company has a power failure. They go into crisis mode and resolve the problem, but they do not assess the damage done. They know that they did not lose any product during the crisis, so they do not document any losses other than production time and labor. Unfortunately, they fail to note that the power outage caused a "brown out," and the irregular voltage destroyed electrical components in some of the manufacturing machinery. This damage could have been avoided if the machinery was turned off, but nobody has been made aware of this fact. This means a power outage could again cause a "brown out" that does the same type of damage to the electrical components of some manufacturing machinery.

- *Information*

    Information is necessary to prevent problems from reoccurring. However, some organizations fail to gather that information...and they end up in the same crisis situation.

    Example: Assume the food processing company has a power failure that puts them in a crisis situation. They determine the power failure was due to a malfunctioning transformer, so they get that transformer repaired. However, they fail to get feedback from everyone involved in the incident. They do not discuss the problem with the power company, and the power company has valuable information that could have been shared. They know that the transformer malfunction was due to water damage from rain, and a simple cover would prevent it from happening again. Without this information, the food processing company will likely encounter the same crisis in the future.

Now you are aware of some of the weaknesses of crisis management programs. These programs are now routinely implemented in organizations, so they need to be improved...and the next section focuses on their improvement.

Improving

Most organizations will face a crisis at some time, and this means they need to be prepared by having some type of plan in place. That plan is known as a crisis management program...something many companies have already implemented. However, one problem with these programs is the fact that they are usually not as good as they could be. In other words, they could use some improvement...and some important suggestions for that improvement include:

Follow the program

This is the most basic suggestion. Many crisis management programs work well when they are accurately followed, but this is often not the case. When a crisis occurs, employees tend to react from instinct and do what they feel is best at the moment. These individuals are in a panic mode, and they make decisions that reflect their panic. Unfortunately, wrong decisions are usually made...and everyone suffers. In short, crisis management programs are developed based on thought and sound principles, and they must be followed in order to be effective.

Clearly define roles

This refers to the crisis management team. If team members are not sure what they need to do, then the program will not be effective. Individual team members need their roles defined so they can take on the responsibilities that go with those roles. When there is clarity, confusion is eliminated and members work together toward a common goal. As noted earlier, lack of communication is a weakness for crisis management programs...and clarity helps eliminate that weakness.

Train the spokesperson

Spokespeople might be gifted writers or speakers, but they can still write or say the wrong things. They need to be prepared to cover the necessary bases and prevent bad information from leaving organizations. This preparation needs to encompass all the necessary "dos" and "don'ts" of communication during a crisis...including the use of social media. The crisis itself is a major problem...and communication mishaps add to that problem. In short, a little time spent training the spokesperson can prevent many problems during a crisis.

Train the trainer

Typically, someone in the organization takes a lead role in training personnel. This trainer makes sure members of the crisis management team understand their roles and he or she oversees all practice runs. Unfortunately, many times the person in the lead role does not have the necessary experience to take charge. If this is the case, organizations need to invest in outside firms that specialize in "training the trainer" for crisis management.

Utilize technology

Technology is constantly progressing, and it needs to be taken advantage of in crisis management programs. For example, cell phones can be equipped with apps that alert team members when crisis situations occur. This is much better than hoping that they are by their computers to receive an email or trying to call or text multiple parties. Another example involves camera capabilities. Activities in organizations can be viewed from any computerized device with internet access, and findings can be used streamline crisis resolution. In short, technology works to identify and resolve crises more efficiently and effectively, and its value cannot be ignored or underestimated.

Look for change

Crisis management programs need to be followed...but this does not mean that they need to remain the same. Organizations always undergo change, and they need to adjust their crisis management programs accordingly. This process should be proactive where organizations are constantly asking what works and what does not. Change takes employees out of their comfort zones, but it is necessary in order to improve crisis management programs. Unfortunately, many people will not accept change unless they are required to do so; and this hinders their personal and professional growth. As one astute business leader jokingly stated, "the only change my employees accept is an increase in their paycheck....and that is only if it does not put them in a higher tax bracket."

Now you understand some ways that crisis management programs can be improved. Let's move on the next section that highlights the importance of crisis management by discussing its role in the future.

Future

Nobody has a crystal ball to predict the future, but it is fairly safe to assume that crisis management programs will become more common in all types of organizations. Some of these programs will be implemented voluntarily, but others will be mandated by government regulations. Crisis situations will arise, and they will need to be dealt with as efficiently as possible.

For food processing companies, crisis management programs likely will be made mandatory by the Food and Drug Administration (FDA), USDA, and state and local health departments. This is due to food safety concerns for the general public. Government authorities do not want to release adulterated or contaminated products into the food supply chain for fear of people getting sick...and possibly even dying.

Summary

More and more leaders are realizing that crisis management is important to the growth and survival of their organizations. This importance will grow in the future, and it means the proper implementation and maintenance of crisis management programs will also become more significant.

This book focuses on crisis management in organizations. It explores different types of crisis situations, shows how to set up crisis management programs, examines the weaknesses of these programs, suggests methods for improving these programs, and discusses the future of crisis management in general. Real world examples are used for illustration and exemplification purposes, and the text is written for easy understanding at any reader level.

Congratulations! You now understand more about crisis management...an increasingly important aspect of planning for organizations all over the world.

Project Management
in Organizations
A Basic Introduction

Louis Bevoc

Published by
NutriNiche System LLC

Introduction

Project management is exactly what it says...it is the management of projects. Obviously, this is an oversimplified statement because there are many variables involved in management, and they all have importance. The following discusses some of the major variables using the implementation of a new pretzel production line at a bakery as an example:

Objective

Every project needs to establish an objective in order to develop a plan of action. The objective of the bakery is to establish a new production line for pretzels. More specifically, this line must be able to manufacture 600 pretzels per hour, or 4800 pretzels in an eight-hour shift. This objective needs to be kept in mind by the project manager (also known as PM) throughout the project to assure it is accomplished. For example, if an engineer determines that the line is only capable of producing 3200 pretzels in an eight hour shift, then the project manager is obligated to stop the project from moving forward until the necessary changes are made to meet productivity standards.

Materials

Materials for the pretzel line project need to be managed, and this involves asking questions. What materials will be needed? Has everything been ordered? When will the materials arrive? Where will the materials be stored? All of these questions need to be answered for the project to flow smoothly. Project managers might not do the actual ordering or inventorying of the materials, but they need to coordinate the overall process. PMs have a responsibility to manage materials, and their failure to do so could bring projects to a screeching halt.

People

People involved in the project need to be identified...regardless of whether they are company employees or contracted workers. Again, this involves asking questions. Who will be needed to complete the pretzel line project? When and where will they be needed? People involved in design, engineering, employee safety, food safety, quality assurance, and testing will all need to be part of the project, and their involvement needs to be managed. Project managers need to tap the expertise of all of these individuals to keep the project moving forward. PMs do not need to do the actual work because the people are qualified to do their jobs, but they need to tell people when and where their services are needed in order to keep the project moving forward.

Time frame

Some projects tend to go on forever, and this is usually is due poor management. Project managers need to establish time frames for completion so people are aware of what they need to do and where they need to be in terms of accomplishing tasks. The time allotted for the pretzel line is 120 day from the start of the project. The required raw materials (ingredients, packaging, boxes, etc.) must be in the bakery 90 days after the project has started, and test product must be run within 100 days. Based on these requirements, product will be ready to hit the store shelves within the 120 day time frame.

Cost

Cost is a factor for most activities in organizations, and it needs to be a factor for the pretzel line. Management has been determined that the total cost for the pretzel line must not exceed $200,000. This includes design, production equipment, installation, and testing. If the cost exceeds $200,000, then the project manager is obligated to stop the project from moving forward until a decision to spend the extra money has been made. For example, the CEO of the bakery needs to sign off in order for the additional funding for the project to be approved.

Evaluation

This is done after the pretzel line project has been completed. Did everything go as planned? Were there major problems? If so, what needs to be changed now and for similar projects in the future? The project manager needs to make sure this does not turn into a "blame game" where people are singled out for problems or mistakes. The goal is to evaluate the project, make improvements, and note changes for the future.

The above example is basic, but it provides a general idea of the major variables that need to be considered when a bakery implements a new pretzel line. There are many other details of these variables that need to be accounted for in the project, but this gives a general idea of what is involved.

Now let's move into the next section that discusses skills project managers need to perform their jobs effectively.

Skills

Many of the skills necessary for a project manager are common sense based, but they need to be highlighted in order to get a better understanding of the position. The following are skills that project managers need to possess in order to perform optimally:

Motivation

This is likely the most important skill because project managers are typically not the direct bosses of the people they have involved in their projects. They cannot tell people what to do and expect them to do it. This means they need to find methods for motivating people to perform...and those methods involve having a good grasp of the following:

Team goals

Project managers need to focus on team goals rather than personal accomplishments. This can be difficult because they know the project is their responsibility, and it has a direct reflection on their abilities. That being said, they are held accountable for failure. However, to avoid failure, they need to make everyone strive for success by emphasizing the team effort and focusing on team accomplishments. They must substitute "we" for "I" in conversations regarding the project, and make people feel like they are more than just a "spoke in the wheel."

Communication

Project managers must be able to communicate. This is understandable because PMs juggle multiple tasks while shouldering the major responsibility for the projects they manage. This communication can be face-to-face, by telephone, or electronic; but it needs to be clear and concise so people must know what they need to do in order to achieve goals and objectives. Additionally, open communication motivates people to perform at higher levels because they understand what is expected of them.

Conflict resolution

The ability to effectively resolve conflict is somewhat rare, but it is an important skill for project managers. There are going to be disagreements between personnel working on any project, and those disagreements can lead to conflict. PMs who work to resolve disputes have a much better chance of being successful....and they lower the stress level for everyone involved. Additionally, conflicts that are not addressed can fester and lead to even bigger problems. Escalated conflict causes people to focus on position rather than principle and personal attacks can result. When this happens, the conflict becomes dysfunctional and the impact on the project is almost always negative.

Compromise

Many problems in project management require "give and take" solutions in order to keep the project moving in the right direction. The ability to compromise is very important for project managers because they have to work with a wide variety of people who all have their own agendas. Comprise is necessary for keeping employees happy...and happy employees typically perform at higher levels.

Emotional intelligence

Daniel Goleman is an American psychologist who is famous for his work on emotional intelligence. He popularized the thinking that it is important to recognize emotions, classify them, and use them to influence people's behavior. People with high emotional intelligence are sympathetic, empathetic, and thoughtful toward others. They also know how temper their own feelings and react rationally to situations that might otherwise involve irrational behavior.

In organizations, managers with high emotional intelligence make better leaders due to the empathy and understanding they have for employees. They create harmony at work and make sound judgments when conflicts arise. They put people at ease, gain trust, and develop positive attitudes that help drive organizations toward missions and goals. When employees feel valued, appreciated, respected, and listened to, they are motivated to help themselves and their organizations become successful.

Project managers need to understand people's professional and personal needs. Like it or not, many people bring their personal problems to work...and this affects their jobs. Those experiencing illness, divorce, death, or financial troubles often cannot leave their problems at home because they are simply too much to shut off for eight hours a day. Project managers need to show compassion and empathy for these individuals in order to get them to cooperate and do their best. PMs need to listen to their worker's needs and respond in ways that make them feel better about themselves and their positions in projects. This results in win-win situations because people are happy and projects get completed efficiently and on time.

Now you are aware of some of the more important skills necessary for project managers. They need to apply those skills at work in order to better perform their job functions. That being said, job responsibilities are the focus of the next section.

Job responsibilities

Project managers are accountable for a variety of different job functions because they oversee projects and the people involved. However, they do have some specific responsibilities, and these are as follows:

Proposing

Projects typically do not get started until there is some sort of proposal. This proposal can be formal or informal, but it needs to define the objective of the project and the direction it will take. Once the proposal is accepted, the project moves into the implementation stage.

Planning

Planning is essentially part of the proposal, but it deserves to be mentioned as a separate responsibility due to the amount of time and effort needed to do it properly. Planning involves a vision of how to go about achieving objectives. Project managers need to establish priorities, allocate resources, implement change, and guide an organization toward defined goals.

Planning can be simple or complex, but the goal is always the same...to provide direction for the project. Project managers' thinking generates ideas for the direction, and planning puts their thoughts into action.

Answers to the following questions provide a basic understanding of project planning:

What is involved?

The following are needed to be defined at the start of project planning:

People

People are needed for a plan to move forward, and the plan needs to specify the number and type of people involved. Complex projects typically require more people due to the greater number of tasks that need to be completed.

The people aspect of planning cannot be overemphasized because employees are the key to making the project work. Care should be taken to choose the correct number of people because too few hinder effectiveness and too many create miscommunication and confusion. The type of people chosen is also critical because the right skills sets are necessary for success.

Resources

Resources including time, money, equipment, and supplies are a required part of planning. Without these resources, plans cannot be carried out and projects will not be completed.

Tasks

Tasks are a part of any type of project plan. They need to be assigned to the people with the skills and expertise to complete them.

How does it work?

The following describe the structure of project planning:

Purpose

First, the purpose of the project needs to be defined. What is expected to be accomplished? What are the goals?

Analysis

An analysis of the project needs to be made to determine the people and resources required for tor the tasks that need to be completed in order to accomplish goals.

Strategy

Once the purpose is defined and an analysis is made, it is time to implement some type of strategy. That strategy must utilize the resources to provide a path that leads to project success.

Why is it needed?

The following explain why project planning is needed:

Forced review

Planning forces people to view the path they are going to take to reach designated goals. It pinpoints areas that might not work or do not make sense based on project strengths and weaknesses.

Milestones

Milestones are achievements made as the plan progresses. As employees reach these achievements, they are motivated to keep working toward the ultimate goals of the project.

Goals

In general, people are likely to jump on board when goals of the project are clearly visible. They understand what they need to do and take ownership of their designated roles.

Who does it affect?

This depends on the size and scope of the project. The number of people affected can range from one person to the many people...including suppliers, customers, and the community. For example, an individual can come up with a project plan for data entry of the entire inventory in a grocery store that he is capable of handling alone. He might start with refrigerated foods, next move to frozen foods, then go to dry goods, and finish with general merchandise. Along the same lines, a large oil company might want to incorporate an environmental protection plan, and this project requires the involvement of every employee, customers, and the community.

It is also important to note that projects usually call for tactical planning because they focus on specific divisions or departments rather than entire organizations.

Costing

Cost is important for virtually any organizational activity, and it certainly plays a role in project management. PMs need to establish a budget from the start, and they need stick to that budget. As the pretzel line example in the introduction of this book indicates, exceeding budgets need approval from higher sources...and getting that approval is the responsibility of project managers.

Managing

This is the most obvious responsibility of project managers because it is stated in their title. They directly or indirectly manage people, teams, processes, and procedures. They have the authority to make changes and are held accountable for failures. They are in charge...and all management functions of the project are their responsibility.

Connecting

This refers project managers' roles as liaisons. They interface with a variety of different people, internally and externally, because they are the main contact for the project. This responsibility requires them to organize every aspect of projects and answer any questions that people ask. They are the major source of information, and everyone involved with projects views them as "go to" people. Not surprisingly, this adds many headaches to PMs' jobs. However, connecting is essential for project completion, and the responsibility for it falls on the shoulders of project managers.

Reporting

Milestones are often part of a project, and project managers are charged with reporting on their successes or failures. This might be a simple as an email or it might require detailed data analysis on a periodic basis...it all depends on the project.

Unfortunately, the completion of projects does not always complete the responsibilities of project managers. Many times they are required to write reports that summarize what transpired and what was achieved. This adds to their workload after everyone else associated with the projects has moved on to other tasks.

Now that you understand the responsibilities of project managers, it is time to move on to the next section that discusses the advantages of project management.

Advantages

Project management is important because it focuses on specific goals within organizations. That being said, advantages provided by project management need to be discussed...and that is the focus of this section.

Project management advantages include the following:

Feedback

Top performing project managers are always trying to improve their projects, and feedback is very valuable for making those improvements. PMs provide stakeholders (people with interest or concern in the projects) with positive and negative information, and that information generates feedback. Stakeholders gladly give their input because they do not want to be kept in the dark about happenings. They make promises to others based on completion of projects, and they cannot keep those promises if there are delays. Having knowledge of delays will not necessarily help stakeholders fulfill their promises, but it gives them the opportunity to explain the reasons for the postponements; and it helps keep them in the good graces of the people who trusted them. In short, feedback is a constructive tool for improvement...and it is plentiful in projects.

Synergy

Synergy results when multiple minds work together to resolve issues. Since the vast majority of projects are made up of teams, most problems are solved using multiple minds. Every team member can exchange thoughts and entertain other perspectives. Each person has unique strengths that add diversity to the team, and the differing viewpoints contribute to the overall effectiveness. The synergy involved improves decision-making and helps the team reach goals within limited time frames.

Anyone who has experienced the power of synergy would most likely agree that teams are important for problem solving. This is why teams play a big role in projects...and it is also why projects are advantageous for organizations.

Roadmap

Project management involves planning that establishes roadmaps for the things that need to be completed in order to accomplish goals and objectives. Roadmaps provide courses of action that reduce the possibility that projects will fail. In short, much of the guesswork involved with change is eliminated in project management because a plan is in place. Unfortunately, many people do not understand the value of roadmaps because they have limited or no experience using them.

Self-monitoring

This might be the biggest advantage of project management because it is directly related to improving quality. Projects that are managed properly have built- in damage control because everyone is held accountable for their work. PMs watch everything and take action when something is not right. This keeps all people involved on their toes, and it raises the bar on quality. Self-monitoring is critical because it makes projects better and reduces the chance for failure.

As might be expected, there are also some negative associated with project management…and that is why disadvantages are discussed in the next section.

Disadvantages

Perfection

Some project managers are perfectionists. They want everything to be properly completed as planned or they are not satisfied. These PMs are often dedicated and hard-working individuals, but they are doing little in terms of productivity. In fact, they are hindering projects with time delays due to their micromanagement techniques. In the end, projects do not get completed on time and stakeholders are upset. Additionally, people working on the projects are upset because they do not like being micromanaged. These professionals have skills, and they want the freedom to use those skills. In short, perfection is a disadvantage of project management that can affect some of the best PMs.

Outsiders

Many project managers have the ability to effectively manage and complete projects. However, they are prevented from doing so due to outside interference from stakeholders. Stakeholders continually ask questions that impede the project progress, and they bombard PMs with suggestions and ideas that force them to defend their decisions and actions. Part of a PM's job involves accommodating stakeholders, but the time and effort spent to do so can be exhausting and somewhat demoralizing. Stakeholders have a right to know how the projects that they have an interest in are progressing, but they also need to let PMs do their job so the work can get completed in a timely manner.

Routine

Some projects follow the same basic pattern from start to completion. This is good because many of the problems encountered are easily solved since they have been dealt with in the past. However, it also produces complacency that is not good. Experienced PMs can become bored due the routine of the work involved. This is not good because they lose their edge in terms of creativity and learning new skills. In the end, projects suffer and so do the managerial skills of the PMs.

Cost

Cost needs to be discussed because it is important. In fact, some people claim that the bottom line is the only line that matters. This means profitability rules over everything else, and money drives the success or failure of organizations. Unfortunately, this thinking often applies to project management. Cost impacts the success of project management and, as might be expected, PMs are held accountable.

Now that you understand some of the advantages and disadvantages of project management, it is time to move on. The next section looks at the future of project management in terms of areas that will experience change.

Future

Without a doubt, project management will play a role in the way business is conducted for a long time. It was important in the past, it is important today, and it will be important in the future. This can be stated with confidence because organizations need to accomplish goals and objectives, and project management is one of the best methods for doing this successfully.

Although project management will be around for many years to come, there will be some changes necessary to meet the demands of organizations, customers, government agencies, and the public. These changes will include the following:

Participation

Project managers will need to delegate more than ever because they will be forced to take on additional responsibilities. For example, they will spend more time making sure projects comply with government regulations that will become more strict and detailed. Terrorism threats, diversity concerns, and monopolistic actions are all examples of reasons why the government will add more requirements. PMs will also spend time making sure the people within the project adhere to ethical standards established by their industry, their customers, and the public. The internet has made it very easy to spread ill will about people in organizations, and those employees' behavior has a direct impact on the perception of their organizations. In short, all project team members will need to perform at optimum levels with minimum supervision because their managers will be needed in other areas.

Strategy

Competition will drive strategic changes in project management...especially for organizations that compete globally. Resources, both internal and external, will become more limited as businesses spread out to grow internationally. This will make project management even more important because it will be relied more heavily upon to contribute to that growth....and it means require project management strategies will need to undergo change. More diverse groups of people will work together to work on problems, and they will need to find solutions using less money and time. This will be challenging, but experienced project managers will overcome the challenge and help their organizations meet goals and expectations. These strategic changes will have an impact on businesses, but they will serve to make projects management stronger than it ever was in the past.

Social responsibility

Not surprisingly, social responsibility will increase in importance in the future. Businesses will be forced to focus on society and the environment, and this will impact project management. PMs will need to manage projects with a sense of transparency so stakeholders and the public are assured that those projects are carried out in ethical, environmentally conscious, and socially responsible ways.

Ultimately, social responsibility will contribute to the bottom line of companies...but not in a negative way like many people might suspect. When people feel comfortable with the actions of organizations, they purchase their products and services and speak highly of them within their own social circles. Business leaders cannot view social responsibility as a drain on resources that will become scarcer over time. Instead, it must be viewed as the beginning of a great opportunity to become more profitable based on a positive perception of organizational accountability.

Skills

Similar to most other professions, the skills of project managers will need to get stronger. This is part of the strategic changes that need to be made in project management, but it deserves to be mentioned as a separate category because the responsibility falls directly on the shoulders of PMs. Leaders of organizations can make project management strategy changes mandatory, but they cannot force PMs to increase their skills. Project managers need to be self-motivated in order to acquire new and diverse skill sets...or they will not be able to meet future expectations.

Work-life balance

Work-life balance occurs when people accomplish job related goals and enjoy life outside of work. As people's lives get busier and more hectic, they begin to realize the importance of work-life balance. Time is limited, and different things need to take priority at different times in life. People need to work in order to sustain a certain lifestyle...but they also need the time to enjoy that lifestyle.

Technology has completely changed work-life balance. People can now work with others from just about anywhere in the world. This means employees do not have to physically be at work in order to perform certain aspects of their jobs because they can telecommute. Telecommuting helps eliminate stressful, costly, and time consuming aspects of people's jobs. Travel, for example, is often minimized with teleconferencing. A 20-hour plane flights is no longer needed to meet people across the globe, and the company saves money on travel costs.

Project managers will be more accepting of telecommuting in the future. They will allow people to work offsite as long as those people are completing the tasks that they are responsible for performing. Task completing will not be a problem because people will be motivated to perform due to the freedom that telecommuting provides.

Work life-balance is important to people, and it saves organizations money. Based on this, there is little doubt that telecommuting will be a part of project management in the future…especially for organizations working on international projects.

Summary

Project management is the management of projects from start to finish. More specifically, it involves managing people, processes, materials, money, and time. It plays a major role in accomplishing organizational goals and objectives, and its importance will continue to grow in the future

This book focuses on project management in organizations. First it explores the skills and job responsibilities of project managers, then it analyzes the advantages and disadvantages of project management, and last it discusses the future of the field. The text is informational and educational, and it is written for easy reader understanding at all reader levels.

Congratulations! You now understand more about project management…a useful process for achieving organizational goals and objectives.